ON THE
ROAD

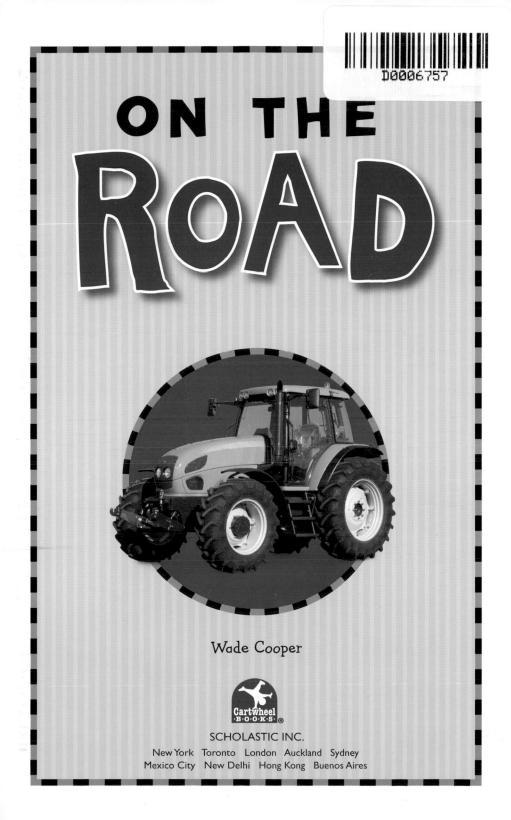

Wade Cooper

Cartwheel ·B·O·O·K·S·®

SCHOLASTIC INC.

New York Toronto London Auckland Sydney
Mexico City New Delhi Hong Kong Buenos Aires

What can you see
on the busy roads?
Cars, trucks, and buses
and tractors with loads.

All moving along,
some fast and some slow.
Do you know what they do?
Do you know where they go?

ISBN-13: 978-0-545-00720-7
ISBN-10: 0-545-00720-8
10 9 8 7 6 5 4 3 2 1   8 9 10 11 12
Printed in China
First printing, January 2008

Reading together

This book is an ideal first reader for your child, combining simple words and sentences with stunning color photography of real-life cars, buses, tractors, and trucks. Here are some of the many ways you can help your child take those first steps in reading. Encourage your child to:

- Look at and explore the detail in the pictures.

- Sound out the letters in each word.

- Read and repeat each short sentence.

Look at the pictures

Make the most of each page by talking about the pictures and spotting key words. Here are some questions you can use to discuss each page as you go along:

- Why do you like this picture?

- What noise does this vehicle make?

- What kind of wheels does it have?

- What job does it do?

Look at rhymes

Some of the sentences in this book are simple rhymes. Encourage your child to recognize rhyming words. Try asking the following questions:

- What does this word say?

- Can you find a word that rhymes with it?

- Look at the ending of two words that rhyme. Are they spelled the same? For example, "roads" and "loads," and "go" and "slow."

Test understanding

It is one thing to understand the meaning of individual words, but you need to check that your child understands the facts in the text.

- Play "spot the obvious mistake." Read the text as your child looks at the words with you, but make an obvious mistake to see if he or she has understood. Ask your child to correct you and provide the right word.

- After reading the facts, shut the book and make up questions to ask your child.

- Ask your child whether a fact is true or false.

- Provide your child with three answers to a question and ask him or her to pick the correct one.

Quiz pages

At the end of the book there is a simple quiz. Ask the questions and see if your child can remember the right answers from the text. If not, encourage him or her to look up the answers.

On the road

What is on
the road?
Turn the page
and see!

The engine in
this yellow car
makes it go –
fast and far.

Go, go, go!

Don't be slow.

Beep
Beep

They roll along
on busy roads.

Honk

Trucks pull
many kinds
of loads

Honk

cab

radiator

wheel

exhaust

11

I'm a mixer.
Here I come.
I mix concrete
in my big drum!

Mix

Mix

Fire truck

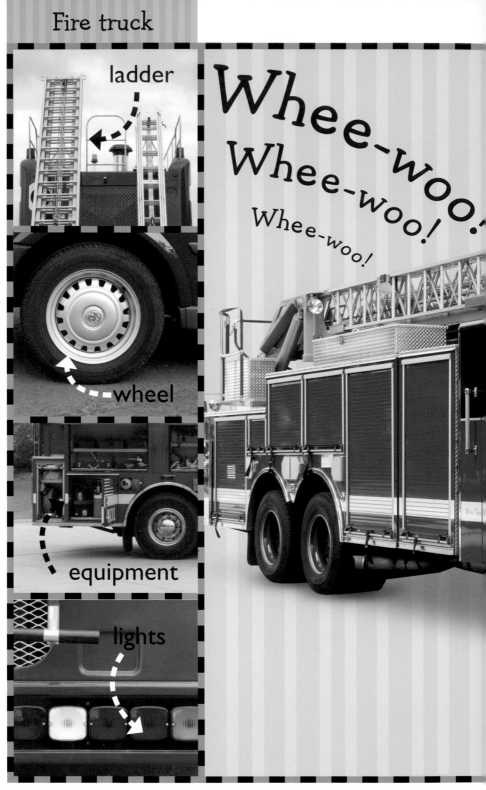

ladder

wheel

equipment

lights

Whee-woo!
Whee-woo!
Whee-woo!

14

"Fire! Fire!"
the people shout.

Here comes a fire truck
to put the flames out.

My arm is long.
My bucket is big.
I was made to
dig, dig, dig!

Dig

Dig

Hear my siren.
I'm on the way.

I will come
to save the day.

Bicycle

helmet

bright vest

Why do I like
to ride my bike?
It's fun to do
and healthy, too.

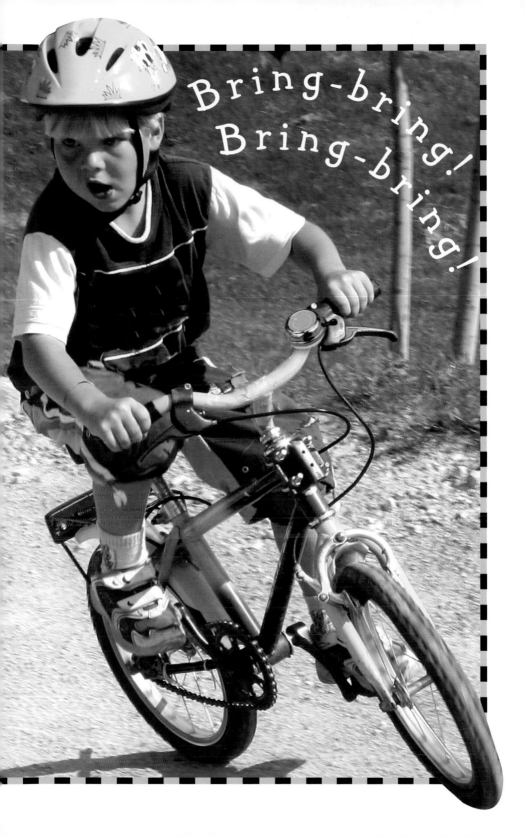

Bring-bring!
Bring-bring!

A motorbike
is fun to ride
through the pretty
countryside.

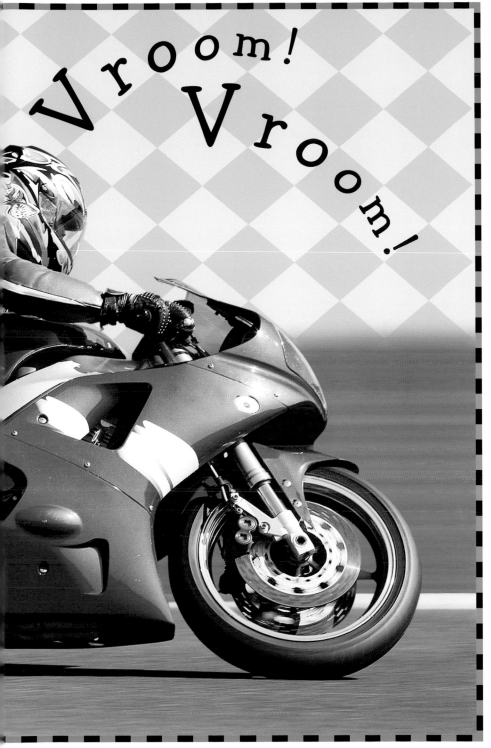

Vroom! Vroom!

It's the big yellow bus
to take us to school.

SCHOOL BUS

All aboard! Move down!
Let's go! Keep cool!

I pull plows and heavy loads on grassy fields and muddy roads.

What do

1. What makes cars go fast?

The engine.

2. What should you wear when you ride a bike?

A helmet and a bright vest.

3. What do tractors pull?

Plows and heavy loads.

you know?

4. Which truck goes
   to put out fires?

The fire truck.

5. How do you know the
   ambulance is coming?

You can hear the siren.

6. What color is
   the school bus?

Yellow.

Useful words

engine
An engine is a machine that uses fuel to make things move.

plow
A plow is a heavy farm tool that turns the soil. It is pulled along by a tractor.

helmet
Always wear a helmet when you ride a bike.

shout
When you shout, you speak loudly.

healthy
Healthy things are good for you.